PROVOKED

to

PURPOSE

Provoked to Purpose

Published by CreateSpace

Tiffany Donald

International Standard Book Numbers:
ISBN: 1540558541 (Amazon paperback)
ISBN 13: 9781540558541 (Glossy paperback)
Cover Image by Bill Hill
Back Cover design by Marlo Halway
Additional editing by Debra Pearson-Matthews
Accompanied by Senator Kevin L. Matthews, of Oklahoma (District 11)

For Information:
CreateSpace Independent Publishing & Platform
North Charleston, SC 29406

Table of Contents

Thanks

THANKS TO ALL OF MY supporters and encouragers!

First, I would like to honor my father, God, for speaking to me many years ago and saying you need to write a book that will encourage many hurting, abused and battered women and men.

Furthermore, I thank God for being with me and my children through every mentioned and unmentioned chaotic experience we have suffered, thus, we are a living testimony of GOD'S MIGHTY HAND! Lord, YOU ARE GOOD ALL THE TIME AND ALL THE TIME, YOU ARE GOOD!

Secondly, I would like to express my love and thank all five of my children; Princeton, Josiah, Jeremiah, Benjamin, and Breanna, for they mean more to me than all the money in the world. Throughout this journey in life, all five of them have been right there and endured MANY hardships with me. Each one of them is like TASTING a special "piece of my momma's homemade lemon pound cake,

(Umm......mmmm GOOD). I love each one of you always and forever!

A Special thanks to my oldest son, Princeton, for allowing the Lord to give him this great TITLE, through a message he spoke at church, for my book. He was the one who encouraged me to walk in my

God-given purpose. Son, now it is your turn. You are an author as well, so *MAXIMIZE YOUR MOMENT!*

Thirdly, I would like to thank all of my family and friends who did not degrade me, rather, acknowledged the extraordinary gifts, talents and abilities to move forward and not faint.

Lastly, I would like to dedicate my book to my father, the late Dr. Bishop John Vincent, Jr., and my mother for all of the prayers and support you have given my children and me. You always could see GREATNESS in me from a small child and now the fruit of your labor is being revealed. I will always love the both of you!

IN MEMORY OF THE LATE BISHOP JOHN VINCENT, JR. - *My Father*

Preface

THE OBJECTIVE AND STIMULUS OF this book is to enlighten, encourage, and inspire each reader to never give up, because many obstacles are inevitable.

Therefore, the world in which we live will create new obstacles every day. However, one must push until change is at the top of their agenda for life, with an extraordinary purpose in mind to fulfill.

To know one's purpose in life, can be quite rewarding. On the other hand, to just exist and not really live is devastating. Someone is watching each of us every single day; thus, living as God has predestined YOU to live will provide many observers the opportunity to acknowledge their need to be motivated and push them towards HOPE.

The scripture says in (KJV) Romans 5:1-6~

Therefore, being justified by faith, we have peace with God through our Lord Jesus Christ. By whom also we have access by faith into this grace in which we stand, and rejoice in hope of the glory of God. And not only so, but we glory in tribulation also: knowing that tribulation works patience; and patience, experience; and experience, hope. And hope makes not ashamed; because the love of God is shed abroad in our hearts by the Holy Spirit who is given unto us. For when we were yet without strength, in due time Christ died for the ungodly.

Introduction

It was a cold winter night in Kalamazoo, Michigan at 8:04p.m., on February 21, 1975; a beautiful milk chocolate, baby girl was born to the union of John and Barbara Vincent. Oh, what a HAPPY DAY! This wonderful couple wanted a girl badly, needless to say, after three tries, here she is! Born with *DESTINY*, born *provoked to purpose* by God.

At about 9 months old, after moving from Michigan to Tulsa, OK, I was in a tragic accident. My family and I were living in a nice apartment complex on the south side of town. One day my mom slipped on an unsecured step as she walked down the stairs, which caused her to stumble backwards down the stairs. I flew out of her hands, over the railing beam, and onto hard pebble rocks.

My mother said she could not get right up at first, because, she was in so much pain. However, she knew she had to check on the baby girl God had blessed her to behold. The last she heard from me was a LOUD CRY.

Finally, she was able to regain her stability and she rushed to check on me. At last, she made it to the site where I had fallen and to her surprise, I was still breathing and conscious. However, I suffered a swollen head and swollen eye. My right eye swelled to the size of an egg. After the doctor completed the examination, my mother later found out that I did not suffer any broken bones or a concussion; nevertheless, she had a miscarriage. This of course, was SHOCKING NEWS!

As time passed, I began to grow and develop in Tulsa, Oklahoma. At the age of about five years old, the gift to sing and captivate the spirit of many was upon me. Although, I was quite shy, yet bold with tenacity, my ability to sing began to open doors for me.

My father, a pastor and great leader, walked in a high position of the clergy with an organization that undergirded and supported annual conventions. This annual event provided an opportunity for me to stand strong, with a powerful and persuasive tone, before thousands of engaged listeners.

Many times, requests were made for me to display my God-given passion, but I was a very shy girl, I would stand and cry. One day I broke out of the hard shell of bashfulness and released a sound that made the congregation come to a complete silence just from doing what I loved---- SINGING!

My parents and four brothers (Terry, Keith, Prentice, and Mark) and one adopted brother (Joseph) acknowledged my gift of singing. I sung while I took showers, on family vacations, at church events, and simply around the house. An enormous part of the day and night, I would sing, sing, and sing!

While developing as a teenager, I served as the Praise and Worship leader and Head Choir Director, for three choirs, at my father's church. I lived an exclusively busy life, a student, an employee, and a musically involved director and singer at my local church.

I have received countless awards for academic honor roll and superb penmanship. During my freshman and senior year of high school, I received a nomination and won, for an Outstanding Student award, as well as, alternate Queen for Homecoming. I was very studious and destined for GREATNESS!

During my senior year of High School, there were many Talent Shows, which allowed me to display my talent. I was no longer viewed as the quiet girl, but the cute girl with a peculiar voice. After singing in one of the talent shows, my senior class mentioned to the board that they wanted me to present a song, of my choice at the Vespers Service, the Pre-Graduation Ceremony, in May 1993. Not only did I execute the perfect song, my father accepted the opportunity to be the motivational speaker of the hour.

After graduating from high school, I decided to pursue my journey of higher learning by attending the University of Tulsa (TU). I attended this university for two years and became acquainted with a young woman named Tina. We became close friends over time. As a Christian, I allowed my light to shine and she saw something different in me that created a bond of sister ship. She knew about God, but she did not know God in a personal way, until I introduced her to Jesus, as her Lord, Savior and Friend. She saw Jesus through my walk, talk, and my life.

Moving into young adulthood, I engaged my spotlight opportunity to set foot in a renowned recording studio, in Nashville, TN. This great landing came about through a close friend of the family, Sam Corley III. He heard my melodious voice at a church service, as well as gazed upon my natural beauty. Thus, he was provoked to provide avenues for my start of musical success, through Big Time Productions. Sam Corley III asked me to present a hard copy of a song of my choosing, preferably something original. I thought, how does he know if I compose songs?

However, I shared with him that I was at work one day and the Lord gave me a song, so I began to write, he replied "May I hear it"? I stood with a SHOCKED look and a big smile on my face and said, "SURE"! The song titled, *"Give Him a Chance"*. I was facing an uncomfortable situation in my life and I needed God to help me through it. Thus, the song *"Give Him a Chance"* was precisely what I needed at that moment. Singing has always been a soothing method for me to relax and find peace.

My two younger brothers, Prentice, Mark, and I went to the church, our homemade studio, and rehearsed! The sound was heavenly! Instantly, we all knew it would be perfect to submit to Sam. Sam received the copy of my original work and immediately, without any hesitation, he stated, "I LOVE IT!" From that day until the final recording time, I was all TEETH! That day of the recording, I told myself, "This Is It", my Open Debut!

My "open debut" presented opportunity for my first compilation disc, at the age of 21. This level of excitement encouraged me to return to the studio. However, I have not pursued this passion due to various phases in life. My objective was to reconnect with Sam, as my producer, but he later passed.

At this time, the Southern Gospel arena meets *Tiffany Nicole Vincent!* A pure, crisp sound, polished with A-1 studio equipment effects and sounds. Mind you, I am not a Southern Gospel girl, rather, a Traditional/Contemporary Gospel singer.

My parents always noticed and appreciated my passion to sing. However, my brothers often became aggravated and offended by my endless singing. Little did they know; God was setting me up to be a blessing to *MANY*! My voice was soothing and encouraging, often producing a message through life-changing lyrics. Some of these songs were original pieces of music, but established recording artists wrote most of the songs.

At this point in life, I wanted to be happily married and begin a family. A dream I envisioned as a young girl. Shortly after completing my compilation disc in Nashville, I met the love of my life, Joseph Melvin Donald, Jr.

Joseph and I dated or should I say, "courted" for about a year. Within that year, we decided it seemed apparent, after communicating at length with one another, that we shared the same love language that connected us.

Holy Matrimony between

Joseph & Tiffany Donald
at Fellowship Church, in Tulsa, Oklahoma
April 25, 1998

I's a Married Now

A LITTLE GIRL THAT MOVED into womanhood was getting married. On April 25, 1998, Joseph and I joined in Holy Matrimony by three pastors, my father, Bishop John Vincent, Jr., my father's former pastor, Bishop Lafayette Davis, and my uncle, Pastor Andrew Jackson, Sr.

To my great surprise, I was expecting our firstborn, Princeton (*The Prince*). He was born in Tulsa, OK at St. Francis Hospital, weighing 7lbs 11oz. Princeton was the most beautiful and alert baby boy I had ever seen. While carrying him, he would flip and twist often. At one of my doctor's visit, Joseph (I called him Joe) and I (He called me T), viewed the ultrasound pictures and we were astonished to see him doing cartwheels, waving his hand, and smiling at us.

Princeton was the happiest baby ever, always smiling with a big KOOLAID SMILE. Even now, he smiles daily. He has even received the nickname, "SMILEY".

I really enjoyed my stay at St. Francis Hospital, until one of the nurses walked in my room one day repeatedly and made me feel very uncomfortable. She would walk in the room and ask every time, "Do you want me to take your baby?" I always said no, because she displayed a weird look through her eyes. Seemingly, she had a plan to take my baby from me for good. I was very weak, after delivering Princeton; I thought she was trying to take advantage. Therefore, I found strength to make a call for my mother to come to my rescue, because Joseph had left the hospital to go handle some business and we did not have a cell phone at that time to communicate.

Nonetheless, my mother came and picked my newborn and I up from the hospital and I later united with my husband, at my parents' home. The next day, we heard on the news that a nurse had traumatically brought harm to an infant. Boy, I am grateful I followed my heart and left!

I awaited this grand opportunity to be a wife and mother, however, it seemed like everything was moving at a swift pace, a little too swift. Being a wife and having a baby was fine, but finding out I was now pregnant with our second child was ludicrous to me. Oh no! I cried, not again! Princeton had just made six months and the news was released---YOU'RE PREGO! PREGNANT? Lord, Help Me!

About two months passed and I had a miscarriage. Joe was sad, but I was glad! Nothing personal against the baby, I just did not want another baby so soon! I am not sure Joe understood. I am the woman; he is the man, of course! He planted the seed, but I was the carrier of the seed.

There were many unexplainable changes, not to mention, physical and psychological changes I had already experienced during my pregnancy with Princeton, and I did not want to revisit those changes so soon. Although, I was not sick with "morning sickness" just the fact of getting bigger was overwhelming.

The Coca-Cola bottle was now moving towards a two-liter. One great thing is I was a healthy conscientious dieter, so I lost all the weight after my delivery. However, I felt after the miscarriage it was time to talk with my husband and find a better way to prevent having more babies so fast, but the result of this conversation was another baby on the way.

During this time, my husband had decided to move the family to Niles, Michigan, about forty-five minutes away from Kalamazoo (My Birthplace). Princeton was a year and a half and the new addition to the family was close to being born. I was eight and a half months pregnant. I was in a strange land, with strange people----not a HAPPY DAY!

Mind you, my husband persuaded me to leave and move to Niles during a crucial time in my life; I was eight and a half months pregnant. I agreed to follow him, as my leader and covering, but to my surprise, I moved from luxury to poverty. Joseph was desperate to make the move but obviously unprepared. There was nothing in the apartment to accommodate our needs or wants. He pulled a 2-inch mattress from his eighteen-wheeler truck, because he was a regional and local truck driver.

Subsequently, we had NOTHING! We did not have a bed, furniture, or table. He later purchased a chair for me to sit. I had to lay on this mattress for comfort, but there was no comfort.

After he would leave for work, I would turn and roll to try to get up off the floor from a very uncomfortable and restless night of very little sleep. Besides, we did not even have transportation, so we had to utilize the LIFT transportation service. Again, he had promised these things before making this big move, but as you can see, he did not keep his PROMISE.

He even made a statement to me one day, by saying, "if you be good I will buy you a bedroom suite." Of course, I thought he was very crazy for saying this. After arguing with him about my disappointments, he begins to speak more by saying, "you are just use to a silver spoon, but you need to know what it is like to suffer". Where is the love, I thought? Subsequently, I met an older woman, Mother

King, who somehow knew my dad and mom through revivals in the Kalamazoo area. Once we started to communicate, we connected, which made me feel a tad better.

In March 2000, another beautiful big baby boy was born. I finally made it to delivery time after having a false alarm two weeks early prior to my new baby's birth. He was born in Niles, MI at Lakeland Medical Center. We named him, Josiah (*The* King), since we had several family members named Joseph. This baby was 8lbs 10oz. Can you say B—I—G? However, if you see him now, he is the total opposite---tall and skinny.

I became quite frustrated after having Josiah (AKA Joey/JO JO), because Josiah's personality was extremely different from his older brother as a baby. Princeton was always smiling and hardly ever cried. On the other hand, Josiah cried, cried, and cried. I was like, what is wrong with this baby? To my knowledge, he was crying because he was unusually hungry and he enjoyed lying under me at all times. Yes, he was and is a "MOMMA'S BOY"! Josiah lavished feeding the natural way and he NEVER fed from a bottle. In fact, at about one and a half years of age I had to pump milk and put it in a sippy cup, because he did not like the texture of the nipple on a bottle. Josiah nursed until he was fourteen and a half months old.

Now that we are settling into our new home, I discovered that my husband and my sons are very important to me. Additionally, I loved my husband so much that I gave up living around my family and an established job, working for a Fortune 500 Accounting Firm, to draw closer to him. Mind you, I was accustomed to working. However, I submitted and served, at his request to become a domestic engineer and stayed home, unemployed, for five consecutive years. My belief was hopefully we could build a love together that will never end.

Many nights I asked myself where am I and why? During both of my pregnancies with Princeton and Josiah, my relationship with Joseph (Joe) was off and on with verbal miscommunications, separations, and cold failing love; nothing as I had dreamt. Depending on one income, at Joseph's request, and unstable job opportunities was becoming abusively unbearable. However, I continued to push with intent to save our marriage.

Furthermore, I was accustomed to a secure and independent way of living and this most definitely was not it! I was now wife and domestic engineer. Who and what did I marry ran rapid through my mind. Joseph, I thought, was a decent man; however, I felt he needed guidance on timing and understanding. I felt he was very controlling and he did not know how to love me the way I desired to be loved. He was most definitely drowning in not knowing how to fulfill the demands and expectations of a wife and family. Many mentors strived to assist him down the right path, but his strong will to do things his way brought destruction to our relationship; due to many misunderstandings, we separated for the ump-tenth time.

I suggested counseling for the sake of saving our marriage and we agreed finally after disagreeing on so many other things. In addition, counseling is designed to bring out the good and bad in order **to reach the** root of the problem. Yes, while counseling, we were getting to the root of our problems, but the issues were never resolved because of the word CHANGE. After visits to several counselors, our serious marital issues were not resolved. I considered, with encouragement from Joseph, to move back to Tulsa. Change does not mean you become useless; rather, it should make you become useful and resourceful. Why? Change helps to develop the intent of the heart, soul, and mind of a person.

In the meantime, I became very withdrawn with being intimate with him because I feared becoming PREGNANT! I began to reject him desiring to have a sexual and intimate relationship with me, because I was tired of feeling STUCK. I had more goals in life besides having children. I desired to return to school and pursue a career that could help us become more financially stable, as a family. Furthermore, Joseph and I were beginning to display more and more signs of incompatibility. Nonetheless, we stayed on this bumpy ride for a little bit longer.

At this time, we were now living in Elkhart, IN. This bumpy ride lasted long enough to end up with the third son Jeremiah- *(The Prophet)*. He was another gorgeous curly haired, long eye lashed, baby boy. He was so pretty that many mistook him to be a girl. However, he was HUGE! This baby was the biggest of all my children, 8 lbs. 12.7oz. Can you say "REAL BIG"? We lived in Elkhart, IN; but we had to commute to Goshen, IN where I delivered this beautiful baby boy.

Two months after Jeremiah's birth, Joseph decided we should move to Muncie, IN. During Jeremiah's younger years, eleven months of age, I decided to leave Joseph, so he could get help on knowing how to take care of a family. About two and a half years had passed when Joseph and I started trying to reconnect and make our relationship a marriage, not just an emasculate wedding so I moved back to Muncie, IN and we tried to embrace celebrating one another, instead of tolerating each other. We thought this was an opportunity for us to begin a fresh start and we channeled our goal towards learning how to connect, as a unit.

The pregnancy of Jeremiah, like the first one, was unexpected too! Prior to this conception, I had strongly encouraged Joseph to use some type of contraceptive to prevent pregnancy and he agreed verbally to not impregnate me. Furthermore, I was so tired of being pregnant, because our marriage was not becoming stronger; rather, falling off the cliff. Again, Joseph had an opportunity to prove that he was not a liar he promised me that he would not impregnate me, but he did not keep his promise. Obviously, he was so engaged into the moment that he did not even think about the fact he was forfeiting his agreement he made with me.

Furthermore, our financial strain was causing a greater level of lack. Now, our food supply was growing smaller and limited. One day, our food supply was so low, while I was pregnant with Jeremiah; I cooked a meal with left overs for Princeton and Josiah. Since we did not have enough food for me to eat as well, I had to bite my nails, chew them, and spit them out to curve my hunger pains.

We later had to rely on food stamps, something I was not accustomed to, in order to survive. Joseph was not home at this time to know what was going on. He had decided to go back to school for a while, the children and I were home alone. During this same night, a strange man, knocked at our apartment door and attempted an intrusion, but with the help of God, I moved as swift as possible to the kitchen and grabbed a butcher knife in case I needed to protect us.

Once again, I did not have a way to communicate with Joseph. I wobbled around the apartment, because I was expecting Jeremiah. I told Princeton and Josiah to go into the bedroom. We were living in a one-bedroom apartment, unlike the two-bedroom we had in Niles, MI. I encouraged them to stay very quiet. Although they were extremely afraid, I reaffirmed that everything would be ok. The stranger finally left after trying for about 10-15 minutes, shaking and knocking on the door.

Because of my condition, I know you are saying by now, YOU ARE CRAZY, and you should have used some type of contraceptive to prevent this reoccurring baby booming season. My reply is; I DID!

However, God saw fit for what happened to HAPPEN, because, *nothing happens just to happen. There is always PURPOSE!*

By this time, I was like my dad and mom; saying, where is my GIRL LORD? Although, I had three boys I really desired a baby girl, as they did. However, after having such a big baby, my desire was diminishing rather quickly. I had to push very hard to have Jeremiah and I lost all motivation to conceive again, just to have a baby girl. I wanted to be done with having babies for good. Although, I knew Joe was going to want to try eventually for that baby girl. However, God knew what we needed and when we needed it. The question was, did we know? Remarkably, having three boys made it easy to pass clothes from one baby to the next; however, we were getting deeper and deeper into financial hardship.

I know you are wondering; are you tired of all this drama? The answer is------YES, I REALLY AM! I was so out done with having babies, arguing, kissing, and making up that I told my husband, STOP bothering me intimately! I do not want any more babies, until we can reach a common ground of agreement in our marital relationship.

This led to more uncomfortable and uneasy disagreements so I moved, again, back to Tulsa. For about three years, he caught the message, because he was not close enough to engage in intimacy with me, due to the distance apart. Then, at the end of three years, he started to plead with me about moving back to Muncie, IN.

After deciding to move back for the last time, he later pleaded with me about having a baby girl. This conversation was not valuable to me at all. At first, I refused and became very circumspect to having intimate relations with him. Oh, yes! This created much strife; however, I felt this was necessary, until a genuine love affair reunion became passionate and affectionate between the two of us for good.

Meanwhile, after seeing an improvement in him being more stable, I finally submitted to being sexually intimate with my husband.

Of course, you know what happened. Yes, I became pregnant and this time with not just one baby, but two. My maternity process was quite different, but I survived until my delivery date.

I was quite embarrassed to inform my family about being pregnant. However, I became strong enough to communicate with my mother, after being pregnant for five months. One day my mother called me and said, "Well it would be nice to have identical twin girls". I replied, "OH NO! That would be too much hair to do and too much drama".

Nevertheless, I had a talk with God with the intent to petition a request with the expectations of him granting it. My prayer, "I know I didn't communicate with you on this one before I engaged into a sexual relationship with my husband, but please Lord, have mercy on me! I did not know when we asked for a girl I would have two babies at once. Since I was not aware that carrying two babies would occur in my life, please allow one to be a girl. She will be beautiful with long hair. Also, please allow the other twin to be a boy, because Jeremiah needs a younger brother, since Princeton and Josiah share a close bond. And please Lord; allow the delivery time to be only two minutes apart, because the other three deliveries and miscarriage involved severe pain."

I called my mother many times, during the pregnancy of carrying the twins and I asked her to pray for me. I felt I was in a dilemma very deep and I needed tranquility, because my medium size family soon grew large overnight.

During my pregnancy, I could not believe I was really having TWINS. I thought at this point, I would need to go to the crazy house, because of the preconceived thoughts of not having enough energy to care for five children and a husband. I already had two toddlers, one knee baby, and now twins. I bellowed! "What kind of mess have I allowed myself to drown in?"

In addition, I had told Joseph when I was about two months pregnant that we needed to start preparing for, I thought, our last single birth by purchasing a baby bed, onesies, bottles, etc. but he replied, "don't worry, we will, we have time." Sadly, his calculation of time was not on point. When the time came for me to visit the doctor before my delivering time, the physician looked firmly and stated, "Joseph and Tiffany you have carried the twin's full term and I suggest you have the babies today, because they are running out of room." The doctor advised Joseph and I that Benjamin's (Twin A) foot was lodged in my pelvic area, and it was extremely necessary for me to deliver so he would not come into this world with a handicap foot.

I was READY to deliver now, but Joseph replied to the doctor that we could wait, because he was not prepared for them to be born yet. The doctor replied, "I understand, however these babies need to be delivered today to prevent harm to your wife and unborn babies." Then, he looked into my eyes and said, "Tiffany this is your body and the decision is ultimately up to you." Joseph did not agree with how the doctor began to communicate directly with me.

However, Joseph decided for the both of us, and we left the doctor's office with frustration and aggravation towards one another. As soon as we arrived to our vehicle and closed the doors, we were verbally fighting like cats and dogs.

Mind you, at my doctor's visit, Twin A (Benjamin) was in the right position to be born; however, the stress from arguing caused him to flip in the breech position. Finally, after ending our arguing session, we decided to return to the hospital and I prepared to have a C-section. This was very disheartening, because I was expecting to deliver the twins naturally. FEAR was gripping me. Hence, I did not feel secure with Joseph emotionally, physically, or mentally. I desired the presence of my mother, because I felt she would make me feel at ease.

Regretfully, she could not be with me at the time, because a member at the church, in Tulsa, had just passed away. I really felt alone, although, Joseph was right there with me. Since he was so frustrated that I had to deliver the twins, he did not say much to me, nor did he make me feel comfortable. He was bitter. Honestly, I felt Joseph had encouraged a threat on my life or he had premeditated an organized crime, because he helped to create unnecessary stress to me and our unborn babies.

This type of pressure could have taken our babies life and me. In addition, I felt he was very inconsiderate and selfish about my current situation. The twins were in the right position to be born naturally, as the others were born, but due to the emotional and mental stress, my body reversed from its state of relaxation. This most definitely made me come to the decision of I am NEVER having children again, especially with him!

On May 12, 2005, the last of the Joseph & Tiffany Donald offspring were introduced to the world, at 6:02pm and 6:04pm, TWINS. We named them, Benjamin and Breanna. Benjamin was 7lbs 14oz and Breanna was 6lbs 2oz. The twins were born at Ball Memorial Hospital in Muncie, IN. My physician told me that I assisted him with making a Guinness record with birthing twins so big.

I also did not have any residue of an ounce of baby fat, on my body. This birthing experience was truly amazing, yet frightening, because of the urgency of the delivery.

Additionally, having a family this size with one income was becoming very stressful. Mind you, I conferenced with my husband and shared my concerns for my need to work and help create a better **way** of life; however, he disagreed. His objective was to provide, love, and care for his family, by using his strategy of a real man. However, he soon found out rather quickly, that his configured way of providing for his family was NOT working.

It appeared that everything was falling apart and our chance to be together, as a family forever, was more treacherous than previous times. Joseph seemingly became overwhelmed with the boiling pressure he was receiving from me and the pressure of not being able to provide enough, as a man. In addition, he seemingly allowed the perspective of others to detour his commitment and covenant to our five children and me.

The twins are now two months old and he decides we need to move to Anderson, IN. By this time, I am just like, this guy is so unstable and crazy, and I cannot continue to follow a blind man who is leading his family into a ditch -Luke 6:39 says, Jesus even spoke to his disciples and said, "Can a blind man lead another blind man? No! Both of them will fall into a ditch". His taskmaster mannerism was no longer accepted, but rejected, which enabled him to reveal his need to be disconnected.

One day, I overheard him conversing with his mother on the phone that he really loves me and he does not want anyone else. He was discussing with her his likes and dislikes about me. Apparently, she wanted someone different for her son and I believe she encouraged him to leave me. However, his response to her sounded like a plea to remain married.

Unfortunately, she appeared to be quite controlling and an over-bearing mother who wanted her son to leave me and supply her needs no matter the expense. She was not concerned that it may cost a husband, a wife, and five children (which equals a family) to be separated for good, because she craved for what we had. A relationship with a husband and children was something she did not have long, because she had divorced twice. Furthermore, I feel, she encouraged Joseph to leave his family, which created a HUGE LEVEL OF LACK IN EVERY AREA OF OUR LIVES.

This level of lack and uncertainty, I believe, drove Joseph to crave for the single life again. After numerous arguments and some silent frustrations, we separated for the final time. Ultimately, in my opinion, Joseph wanted OUT OF THIS RELATIONSHIP so he encouraged me to leave because he claimed, "We are going down two separate paths." Of course, I thought he was totally insane, for choosing such a time. We did not have one or two children, rather a full squad for a basketball team. However, I began to focus on knowing that these five children are gifts from God. Granting his wish and request, I moved out with nowhere to go! Where is PURPOSE?

Journal 1
(I's a Married Now)

Why do you want to be married?

_____

_____

_____

_____

Are the two of you compatible?

_____

_____

_____

_____

Does your potential soul mate love God, their parents, and siblings?

_____

_____

_____

_____

What are you willing to offer to the relationship that will build a foundation, and reflect stability?

_____

_____

_____

_____

Prayer of Purpose:

(NLT) Hebrews 13:4~
Give Honor to marriage and remain faithful to one another in marriage. God will surely judge people who are immoral and those who commit adultery.

(KJV) Mark 10:9~
What therefore God hath joined together, let not man put asunder.

~NOTES~

CHAPTER 2
Pushed into Purpose

I PACKED ALL OF MY children's belongings and mine. Remember, the twins are two months old, Jeremiah is three, Josiah is four almost five, and Princeton is six almost seven. This was most definitely an awful and awkward position to behold.

I had just given birth to twins and my body had not healed. However, I pushed through the physical pain (from the Caesarean, with the twins, unlike the three other natural births) and I pushed through the emotional terror, because I HAD TO MOVE! Mind you, Joseph had just moved us from Muncie, IN to Anderson, IN. Sadly, we had to move again, but this time it was to a brand new city and state, Forth Worth, TX. HESITATION CAN KEEP YOU FROM REACHING YOUR DESTINATION! JUST MOVE!

My oldest brother, his wife and family, had a lucrative Daycare business. They needed someone who they could trust and depend upon to push the business into a bigger project of success. That person resembled me--------PURPOSE! I communicated to God again to receive His direction for me and my family. Finally, I realized that sometimes God has to separate you to elevate you! He did just that!

Later, my mother, my eldest brother and his family drove from Texas to Indiana to move my children and me to Texas. We left Joseph behind at his request. My mother knew this was extreme pressure, so she encouraged me to REMEMBER, "God knows and he cares all about me!"

My sister-in law had previously spoken to me several times, by telephone, about moving to Texas, to help elevate their business to another level. At this point, it was quite apparent that Joseph and I were not reconciling our differences, nor agreeing with the same rhythm. I thought things over and spoke to God for direction. I often knew that Oklahoma was my real home! Instead of moving to my hometown, I agreed to move to Texas.

I did not quite understand or even know how to prepare myself for the new challenges ahead; however, I knew that remaining at a stagnated position was NOT AN OPTION!

Journal 2
(Pushed into Purpose)

What or Who is your biggest obstacle? Why?

_____

_____

_____

_____

_____

Are you your own obstacle?

_____

_____

_____

_____

_____

How do you plan to conquer your obstacle(s)?

_____

_____

_____

_____

Are you afraid of your obstacle(s)? If so, why?

_____

_____

_____

_____

_____

Prayer of Purpose:

(NIV) Romans 8:31,32,37:[31] *What, then, shall we say in response to these things? If God is for us, who can be against us?* [32] *He who did not spare his own Son, but gave him up for us all—how will he not also, along with him, graciously give us all things?* [37] *No, in all these things we are more than conquerors through him who loved us.*

~NOTES~

_____

_____

_____

_____

_____

_____

_____

_____

_____

_____

_____

_____

_____

_____

_____

_____

_____

_____

_____

_____

_____

_____

_____

_____

_____

_____

_____

_____

_____

CHAPTER 3

The Transition

MY BROTHER AND HIS FAMILY have a lovely home, but it was not quite spacious enough for eleven people, my six and his five. This metamorphosis we endured for six months and then it was time to create a nest for all my little birdies.

At the end of 2005, embracing 2006, my children and I moved to our new home, in Arlington, TX because it was in proximity of where my new employment was located. Both families were glad to have more space and continued working together, as well as, attending the same church where my brother served as senior pastor. Now, I had to learn how to be a true SURVIVOR, because I was not receiving consistent financial assistance from Joseph at all. In fact, our phone conversations were bare minimum, due to overrated arguments and opinionated personalities.

My sister-in-law began to sit down and discuss my new schedule in life. I was not certain of all the new demands that were ahead of me. As a result, I went into them blind-sided and fearful. I knew God would take care of my children and me, but I did not know exactly how he would do it or even when it would happen.

Of course, this should not have been a concern because GOD IS GOD, yet I am HUMAN! It is always good to know when you place things in God's Hands, He has the BEST HANDS to handle any situation you encounter. For example, I moved to Texas without a job, home, or income. Nevertheless, I relied on my sensitivity to God's voice and direction for my family and me. It was not always easy, but God ALWAYS brought me to an ease. I have learned that if you TRUST HIM, he will GUIDE YOU. However, if you DENY HIM, you will not RELY ON HIM! This will cause your life to experience much strife, pain, and grief. The lack of God's wisdom, knowledge, and understanding for your life pushes you to forfeit your rights to an abundance of blessings; thus, you embrace cursings.

During this transition in my life, I felt angry, frustrated, mad, furious, and forsaken, but I never gave up on God. I knew he had a plan for me, although, I could not see it right then. The only thing left was to TRUST HIM, because, the one I thought would never leave or abandon my children and I; did just that. This is when FAITH and HOPE moved into the driver's seat, forcing DESPAIR and DISAPPOINTMENT to be ran over.

Moving to a new geographical area was different and discomforting, but with the help of God, family, and other support groups, I was able to make the necessary adjustments to remain in the WINNING CIRCLE.

CHAPTER 4

Switching Lanes

~⤴~

Now, I am the Head of Household, not just a wife and mother. At this time in my life, my mind is running 1,000 miles per second. My prayer is, "Lord, help me not to give up so I can fight for me and my children."

I began my work schedule at the Daycare, providing my services where needed. This conversion from domestic engineer for five years, to a working mother of five was kicking me right dab in the center of my rear. I thought I was ready to take on more multitasking positions, but I soon discovered even more weary and tired nights.

I was now waking up at 4:45am every morning to prepare my family for a day of work. Every morning was a hassle because the children were very sleepy and cranky, they would cry all morning long. On top of that, Josiah would have asthma attacks often. Can you say, STRESSED? In fact, one of Josiah's asthma attacks caused him to be hospitalized, due to him contracting pneumonia. We did not have transportation, so we had to contact a cab service to assist us. The cab driver was so sympathetic towards our situation that he offered to be our chauffer at a very feasible fee. He stated, with empathy, "I feel your pain, because you are handling five children and managing to walk sanely by yourself. You are a strong woman."

In addition, we had to walk to work and church most of the time. However, a friend of mine, Phyllis, would often assist me with grocery store visits on days when I did not walk to the grocery store. All five of my children would whine because I was working a split- shift, 6:30am to 6:30pm and in the summer months, Texas feels like a million plus saunas. However, we would not leave until the last parent picked up their child. Many times the last child left after 7pm.

Can you guess what I had to do? Guess? I had to develop a system so I could handle ALL of my demands a little better. Already over ex- erted my new system consisted of preparing my meats at night, while the older three took turns bathing.

Princeton, being the oldest, assisted very well with making sure this task was completed. Then, I would come home on my lunch hour and finish preparing the sides for dinner. Some days I rested on my lunch break, however, many days I cleaned the house and made sure that dinner was completed and ready.

We arrived home many nights between 7:30pm and 8:00pm. A little elderly white woman would watch our going and coming, as our personal bodyguard.

This chaotic schedule went on for three years, until I realized and heard God say, I needed to move on to Oklahoma and continue the fight.

Many nights I would have dreams of devastating events. I spoke to God about it. The Lord gently said, "It was time for me to move on to Oklahoma". I obeyed the voice of God and moved.

A few months before moving, a great man by the name of Bishop Tommy Riddle, gave me a car so we would no longer have to walk to church, work or the grocery store. He respected me as one of his very own daughters and I considered him as an interventionist. He knew about my plans to move back to Oklahoma and he was eager to assist. He, his wife, and my mother drove to Texas and assisted my family and me with our move. This time, I was independent and financially secure to move. The Lord allowed great finances, almost $8,000, to come to my household unexpectedly at that time, by mail, prior to this move. After moving back to Oklahoma, a few years later, Bishop Riddle passed away.

Upon my return home, many family and friends were shocked to see my weight in total control, as well as ecstatic to greet my family and me. I was accustomed to being a size 9/10; however, I had dropped down to a size 5/ 6. I did not carry any baby fat while carrying the twins, so I lost weight tremendously. Although, my body is physically fit, I was mentally and emotionally exhausted. Nonetheless, I persevered through this additional transition in our lives.

My dad and mom were honored to have us home. I am the only daughter to my parents it was quite a strain for them to observe the uncomfortable situations that had occurred so frequently in my life, while living many miles away. However, all this drama was leading me to PURPOSE!

Journal 3 & 4
(The Transition/Switching Lanes)

Are you ready to embrace change?

_____

_____

_____

_____

_____

_____

What is holding you back from change?

_____

_____

_____

_____

_____

How do you handle pressure?

_____

_____

_____

_____

_____

Are you afraid to become a better YOU?

_____

_____

_____

_____

_____

Prayer of Purpose:

(AMP) Psalms 139:16
Your eyes have seen my unformed substance; and in your book were all written the days that were ordained for me, when as yet there was not one of them.

(NASB) Daniel 2:21
It is he who changes the times and the epochs; he removes kings and establishes kings; he gives wisdom to wise men and knowledge to men of understanding.

~NOTES~

CHAPTER 5

The Journey

JUNE 2007, HERE WE ARE again, starting at the bottom, I thought. However, my parents were glad that I was in one piece after all I had experienced. Although, I had experienced much HELL on earth, "I didn't look like what I had been through"! My parents gladly welcomed my children and I home. We were now a part of their household, just temporarily, even though I was clueless on how I would create another new home for the six of us.

By this time, I was perplexed, yet, determine to reach my God-given purpose. For me to experience all this drama, I knew God must have Purpose somewhere waiting for me. My children and I resided with my parents for a few months until the door of opportunity kissed me on my lips. The children are now a little older; Princeton-9 ½ years old, Josiah-7 ½ years old, Jeremiah-5 ½ years old, and the Twins (Benjamin & Breanna)-2 years of age.

At this time, I decided counseling for my three older children and I was needed. Since the twins were so young, the counselor made an exception for them. Moreover, the older boys always told me that the counseling sessions never helped because I would utilize my own gifts, talents, and abilities to have special meeting times with my children for them to release, talk, or vent their concerns. I believe they felt more secure with me versus a complete stranger, who was not connected to our present situation. In addition, they felt the love and strength I had naturally and spiritually to push, in spite of, helped more than anything did. Furthermore, we all realized that the spiritual stability of my faith, in God, brought us through.

My children were mind boggled by the scores of promises that Joseph had made to them at a young age and did not keep. Devastation most definitely knocked us out the front door through the back door. For example, Joseph promised to NEVER LEAVE US and ALWAYS be there for his family. This involved taking care of his family in every way possible. He told the older boys, Princeton and Josiah that he would advise and coach them with their basketball interest as they grew into their teenage years. These were all promises that never happened.

My father and mother owned a property, five minutes away from their current home, where I grew up on Fairview Street in Tulsa. It was vacant at the time of our move, but I was not financially ready to adjust. However, one day my mother and I were talking and the phone rang. The call was from one of my younger brothers, Prentice. He and his wife, Kenya, had just added a new member to their family, a baby girl, Korbyn.

My brother and his wife needed someone to care for their baby, so they could return to work. He spoke to me and offered to pay me for being a caregiver for his daughter. I gave it a long thought, because, I have five children of my own and I was not quite ready to deal with crying and feeding a newborn on the hour all over again.

However, I finally agreed, after consulting with God and I needed income. Since Joe was not consistent again with child support, I had to apply for housing assistance and food stamps. This was something new to me. I had ALWAYS BEEN INDEPENDENT. I felt so embarrassed and humiliated! Hence, I realized quickly, as my mother says often, "I have to accept what God has allowed".

September 2007, I began to provide care for my niece at the home on Fairview Street where we were now living. This brought in very little income, some money was always better than NO MONEY AT ALL. Child Support was starting to come in more regularly, however, for five children it was not quite enough income to survive on my own.

Therefore, the journey begins and continues when suddenly my first cousin, Terrence, called and stated he had heard that I was providing care for my niece and he needed the same care for his daughter, Terran. I listened carefully and went back into my prayer closet to see if I was about to dig a deeper pit for myself. I already had so many demands. After given it some thought, I agreed. Shortly after, I ran into friends of the family, Tim and Erin by way of Prentice, at our church garage sale.

This young couple had a 10-month old son, Jonathan, and needed a caregiver as well. Somehow, they received information about my services and I was now providing what I had to offer to the community. They knew after a short conversation that our meeting was divine, because they had just spoken to one another about locating someone they could trust to watch over their baby. Their goal was to find a good daycare, so they could work together on their established business, selling cell phones and other electronic devices.

They finally asked the big question, "Can we start soon, please count us in?" I smiled, and of course, I agreed. I knew at that very moment that God was opening a door for me to have a small in-home Daycare business that would take care of my family and me. On top of this, I started receiving child support more regularly, in fact, every week for about one year. HALLELUJAH!

My experiences with my own children and the Daycare children in Texas had made me very efficient, effective, and qualified. Furthermore, my small daycare business was not in my original plans, however, God allowed PURPOSE to embrace me once again.

Children began to come from left and right, because I displayed obedience to the focus and direction of God for my family's life and me. This job was no longer a babysitting position, rather, an evolving business and outreach ministry for those in need and the hurting.

Many days I had to encourage and minister to some of the parents, because they were facing many obstacles, frustrations, and disappointments in their own marriage, relationship, and just life. My struggles and experiences in my life made me an example of God's Grace and Mercy!

Some couples were on the verge of a divorce, but God allowed me to intervene and encourage them through my life experiences and wisdom. Subsequently, things began to expand quickly. I was offering HOPE through my provided daycare services and my life experiences that enabled me to have wisdom and motivated discernment.

Therefore, I decided to become a certified caregiver with the State of Oklahoma. I operated this business, like a well-established, lucrative corporation. My objective was to provide for my family, without a financial fight. This opportunity gave me the financial freedom needed to swim above water and not drown. Not only did I set myself up to pay my own bills, I was also able to assist others, including my parents.

During this time of soaring like an eagle, Joseph begins to contact the children and me more frequently. Although, we were not living in the same home, we were legally married. Sooner than later, another blowout occurred, causing him to stay away until a divorce was FINAL!

October 26, 2009, to my surprise I received divorce papers. I actually thought they were forged documents, because Joseph and I had just communicated in an extensive, sexual way and through conversation that we wanted our marriage to live, two months prior to this devastation.

In fact, he came to our home to visit the family with intent, he said, to reconnect and move forward. In addition, Joseph stated that he had planned for a divorce back in June of 2009, but he revoked his request. However, according to the court clerk, these were legal documents without my signature. Obviously, he did not follow through with his revoking request for dissolution of our marriage.

Subsequently, this shocking bad news was an unwanted reality! I really did not know how to respond and I felt very lost for words. My parents were married for almost 50 years and I dreamt that Joseph and I would be a union until death parts us; in spite of, our need to be unified. Unfortunately, this was not the case; I felt betrayed.

This final blowout served as an unexpected end to our union and a pursuit of unhappiness. Although, Joseph stated many times he wanted his family and none other, his actions displayed something very different, in my opinion.

I was always told if you want something bad enough, you FIGHT for it; it is apparent he chose to LOSE.

Pushing into purpose, I continued to strategize the layout of my small business. In spite of the many obstacles, I faced. I even decided to pursue happiness by returning to school, so I could acquire my degree. These two options were the best decisions I settled on.

One of my strategies for my daycare business was to offer something most daycare providers did not provide, a home-cooked meal. For example, one meal consisted of tilapia fish, mixed greens, field peas, fruit, and cornbread. This type of meal and many others like it, assisted with keeping my daycare children enrolled, with a healthy immune system daily. The food was so tasty that the parents requested I begin a carryout service for them; however, this time I declined.

Additionally, the option of pursuing the daycare business allowed me an open window to spend quality time with my own children, as well as others' children. I needed this quality time spent with my children, because we had all suffered so many negative experiences. However, generating three incomes at this time was the sign of PURPOSE! Finally, we were now dwelling in PURPOSE, not POVERTY!

Journal 5
(The Journey)

How do I reach my goal(s)?

_____

_____

_____

_____

Rate where you are on your journey? (Circle the number)
(Rate from 0 to 10) 0-4=Excellent, 5-7=Fair, 8-10=Need to Improve

Organization	*0 1 2 3 4 5 6 7 8 9 10*
Patience	*0 1 2 3 4 5 6 7 8 9 10*
Consistent	*0 1 2 3 4 5 6 7 8 9 10*
Procrastinator	*0 1 2 3 4 5 6 7 8 9 10*
Persistent	*0 1 2 3 4 5 6 7 8 9 10*
Low self-esteem	*0 1 2 3 4 5 6 7 8 9 10*
Inadequate	*0 1 2 3 4 5 6 7 8 9 10*

Do you have a healthy support system? (Remember~ **Everyone is not your confidant)

List your Support Group members:	*List non-Support Group members:*
	(Make sure you put an X on this list)
_____	_____
_____	_____
_____	_____
_____	_____
_____	_____

Prayer of Purpose:

(GW) Philippians 3:13-16: Brothers and sisters, I can't consider myself a winner yet. This is what I do: I don't look back, I lengthen my stride, and (14) I run straight toward the goal to win the prize that God's heavenly call offers in Christ Jesus. (15) Whoever has a mature faith should think this way. And if you think differently, God will show you how to think. (16) However, we should be guided by what we have learned so far.

~NOTES~

_____
_____
_____
_____
_____
_____
_____
_____
_____
_____
_____
_____
_____
_____
_____
_____
_____
_____
_____
_____
_____
_____
_____
_____
_____
_____

CHAPTER 6

Determined

DURING THIS PUSH TO PURPOSE, May 2010, I returned to college, as a full-time student. Yes, I was still operating my daycare business full-time as well. Josiah, my second son, began to have recurring asthma attacks that eventually hospitalized him, this time for two weeks.

I cried, OH GOD! This added pressure is very intense, however, I continued to work and provide for my family. Josiah had to be in the hospital primarily by himself, until the daycare closed at 5:30pm. Moreover, my dad, mother and brother, Mark, adjusted their schedules when available.

During my workday, Josiah would call me and I called him sporadically throughout each day. The weekend was the only time I could be with him all day and night. Most times he called and asked, "MOM, when are you coming"? I would reply, "Soon just wait for me". His reply would be, "Ok." We ended every call with I Love You!

I had to explain to him, mommy had to work so I could provide for the family. This was very difficult and scary for Josiah, for me as well. He was a young child surrounded by strangers most of the time in a sick place, the hospital. Of course, as a mother, I felt very uncomfortable, and I always questioned him to make sure NO ONE was harming him in any kind of way!

As soon as I thought the pressure was subsiding, it appeared to multiply. I almost gave up, but PURPOSE was calling me! Many family and some friends encouraged me to push, especially my Aunt Princess and a good friend, Lance. Although I had been divorced for one and a-half years, I kept pushing right into PURPOSE!

June 2010, I purchased a Chrysler Town & Country (Limited Edition) mini-van, the family's vehicle. I was able to pay cash money with a zero balance. The children and I were very excited! We shouted and danced for days up and down the street, in our neighborhood, as well as, my parent's neighborhood. This vehicle was a leap of faith from walking to riding. We did not just ride in anything, but we were riding in style, without a shame face.

For a while, I had to drive one of our church vans; because the vehicle Bishop Riddle had given me was beginning to slowly, but surely decline in functioning properly. The church van was a huge gas-guzzler and many of the homeless people recognized the van, with a desire for me to give them a ride. They had become accustomed to my father driving the van. Sometimes, they would run up to the van, not knowing who was driving, demanding a ride. However, when we purchased our minivan, we no longer had to deal with acknowledgment by so many homeless people. I did not mind helping people; however, I had to be extremely careful because my children were still quite young. Besides, they were cautiously adjusting to our new life in Tulsa, because their father had moved us around so many places.

This vehicle was reliable for me to race back and forth to school, church and anywhere else, I needed to go. I even travelled many places out-of-town in this vehicle. My sigh of relief had come. I called Joseph, told him about Josiah's situation, and demanded his attention for the sake of our son. He made many excuses about his job, until he heard a certain resounding noise from my lips. This sound placed his ears at attention. He soon arrived and rendered his services to our son. I felt at ease and went home to rest. Josiah is released from the hospital; finally.

In the same year, a friend of mine, Laura, by way of OKC, OK invited me on a special trip. I had just spoken aloud to myself that I need a BREAK! I believe God heard my despair and decided to rescue me. My friend, invited me to attend a seven day cruise (Half Moon Cay, Bahamas/San Juan, Puerto Rico/St Thomas, Virgin Islands/ and The Grand Turk-Caicos), and I agreed. I had dreamt of a cruise since I was a little girl. Now, one of my dreams was finally coming true!

This trip was a well-needed break; however, I missed my five children by the third or fourth day. We were not accustomed to being apart from each other. In addition, I knew I had to get back soon because I was working on completing my degree in Business. Due to various roadblocks, my goal to complete school has yet to be reached; nevertheless, I was pursuing my opportunity to resume my goals and objectives. As a result, I continued my studies until I graduated December 2012. This was indeed a HAPPY DAY!

Coming to the close of five years with my daycare business, I decided to close for good. I felt God had something so much "bigger and greater" for me. Therefore, I walked another mile or two on this journey. All the daycare children were finally growing up and no longer in need of my care. However, it was now time for them to move on to their time in life of promotion, from newborns to early childhood development. At this point, I made a decision to pursue a position of employment outside of my four walls.

Journal 6
(Determined)

What do you plan to do with your life now?

_____

_____

_____

_____

Are you ashamed of your mistakes?

_____

_____

_____

_____

Do you make sound decisions or hasty ones? Why?

_____

_____

_____

_____

_____

Prayer of Purpose:

(KJV) II Timothy 1:7
For God has not given me the spirit of FEAR; but Power, Love, and a sound MIND.

(NIV) Psalms 40:12
For troubles without number surround me; my sins have overtaken me, and I cannot see. They are more than the hairs of my head, and my heart fails within me.

(NASB) Psalms 19:12
Who can discern his errors? Acquit me of hidden faults.

~NOTES~

CHAPTER 7

The Land of Opportunity

JUNE 2012, I HAD THE blessed opportunity to take my children on a 3-day cruise to Nassau, Bahamas. Before boarding the ship at the Port, we spent a day at The Holy Land in Orlando, Florida.

I made many promises to my children and this was one that I kept, (like all other promises, I had made to them). Being a woman or man of YOUR WORD is your BOND. From this revelation, I decided to open the family vacation getaway to my extended family members, after hearing God say, "Ask your father and mother to go with you and your children". Also, open up the family vacation to other family members."

Nonetheless, my dad, mom and oldest brother and his family were the only family members able to join us on this trip. God tremendously blessed me that year with financial security, so I offered and paid for my parents' entire getaway excursion.

There are so many fond memories from this trip. I later found out even this trip had PURPOSE! My desire was to stay close to my children, although, time was moving and my babies were sprouting.

One day, through the great advice and mentorship of my mother, I applied for a job at the Tulsa Education Service Center. Somebody say P-U-R-P-O-S-E? Upon picking the twins up from school one day, I visited with a few friends and associates of mine. We begin to communicate for a lengthy time. While chatting, the principal asked me, "What are you doing these days"? I replied, "Well, I just closed my in-home daycare business and I'm searching for new employment opportunities."

My goal is to do all I can, since I am doing it solo. She replied, "Really? Your husband left you"? I stated, "Yes and no, he requested me to leave and I honored his request. He is no longer around so I am left with five children to raise alone."

The shocking news almost placed her into a coma. She quickly sympathized and empathized with her response, "I have a spot for you". I pursued this opportunity the next day.

This position allowed me to serve as a TA (Teacher's Assistant) and Music Facilitator for the girls and boys who enjoyed expressive dance and singing. I know this position was not quite what I desired, because the pay is less than what I was accustomed to receiving, but I realize that sometimes you have to go down to go up.

I had the best time working with four wonderful, black, educated women. One of the women was my 6th grade Reading/Math Teacher, Mrs. Harris. This team knew how to make a person feel comfortable, so the adapting process did not take as long to build new relationships; the pleasure was all mine!

I continued with this journey, until I received a new assignment, through the Tulsa Education Center to a new location across Tulsa. I decided to decline on my new job placement because my adjusted income was not economically feasible and the commute was too far. Suddenly, during this 2012 school year, my father suffered with a chronic illness.

Journal 7
(The Land of Opportunity)

Are you ready to adventure out?

_____

_____

_____

_____

_____

Do you like to take risk? Why or Why not?

_____

_____

_____

_____

_____

Are you sulking in your past mistakes or current disappointments?

_____

_____

_____

_____

_____

Prayer of Purpose:

(NKJV) Proverbs 3:5, 6
Trust in the Lord with all thy heart and lean not unto your own understanding. In all your ways acknowledge him and he shall direct your path.

~NOTES~

_____

_____

_____

_____

_____

_____

_____

_____

_____

_____

_____

_____

_____

_____

_____

_____

_____

_____

_____

_____

_____

_____

_____

_____

_____

CHAPTER 8

The Open Door

THROUGHOUT THE (2012) SCHOOL YEAR, I had to race back and forth to the hospital. This of course, was all new to me. I had never seen my father so weak and feeble. He was always a vibrant, tenacious, and an optimistic man. Seeing my dad at this weak and feeble state was becoming more and more challenging, however, I remained strong to honor and serve him, as Ephesians 6 says.

Time was passing, thus, my father grew weaker. During this process, I placed total trust in God. My father had a look in his eyes that said he was not going to make it. Finally, May 23, 2013, after being very sick for a short time, he passed, *the Late Bishop John Vincent, Jr.* It felt like an awful nightmare, but reality soon kicked into place.

My aunt, Teresa, his youngest sister, and I stayed with my father until he took his last two breaths. I promised him, one day he was talking to me, that I was going to make it to the top and he replied, "I believe in YOU and I love you"! He said, "Tiffany, I am very proud of you. You are a courageous and strong Woman of God!" This transition was quite difficult to bear, but purpose was following me.

Now things are up into the air! Decisions…Decisions…Decisions, I had to assess. I felt the need to speak things over with my mother, so she could sell the house where my family and I were lodging, because she needed us and we needed her, at this transitional time in our lives.

Finally, a potential buyer came along, so we could transfer our belongings back to her big house. We were already spending many nights with her while dad was very ill, however, we had no idea that we would return to reside as residents again.

Time is passing. I need more income to purchase a more reliable vehicle for my family. The van was accommodating for the family, however, the transmission was slowly ceasing to function properly. It drove fine, but it was dying too!

The new school year, 2013-2014, was quickly approaching and nothing was in its proper place. I needed better transportation, but reality said; you need better money too! Soon after, a job opportunity came my way. A friend of mine, Donna, informed me of a teaching position at a local Charter School.

I decided to apply and the response was a MIRACLE from GOD! I received an opportunity to work as a First Grade Teacher on the spot! I was in TOTAL SHOCK! The hours and money were both sustainable. I had tears of joy and sorrow, because my father and I had previously discussed my possibilities while he was ill. He was not here to experience my accomplishment, but I had the opportunity to enlighten him, before he passed. Although he was ill and did not say much, he always smiled whenever I did communicate with him and he looked at me, with deep passion of love, from a loving father to his daughter.

My father was an educator, preacher, pastor and leader, along with many other great things. My dad taught my siblings and me to reach our goals, not just dream them. At that very moment, I thought to myself, I am real close to the Jackpot---PURPOSE! I began my first year of teaching and experienced a wonderfully, exceptional time.

A week and a few days, before my birthday, February 2014, I was able to purchase a more reliable vehicle, a Dodge Journey (Limited Edition). This vehicle was fully loaded. My children desired a TV and many other amenities. I stated to them while we were waiting to purchase a newer vehicle, "Make your request known to God." These children petitioned their wants to the Lord and received an ANSWERED PRAYER. Purchasing another vehicle was an anticipating wait, because we used to walk to my job, church, and sometimes the grocery store, before we were able to invest in a vehicle. Having a vehicle kept a spirit of joy resonating on the inside, as a reminder, that we will not have to walk unless we desired to do so.

Things are looking up for us and we are very happy. Then on April 13, 2014 my mother, my youngest brother—Mark, and my son Josiah, were in a head on collision. The other driver had taken a drug called Xanax and apparently he had fallen asleep at the wheel.

The driver was pushing between 70-80mph at the time of the impact. I was trailing them with my other four children in the car. We saw everything as it occurred; it appeared to be fatal and we thought that all of the passengers were killed at the scene.

What a catastrophe, I thought. My children and I were screaming fiercely without an expected end. I could not believe what we, had just witnessed. As a result, I parked the vehicle in the middle of the street, and ran in my tall heels, with my children, to check on my family.

Did they survive was the question! We had just left a powerful church service and we were ready to dine sufficiently, but little did we know, we were not going to do that at all. Thanks be unto God, everyone survived; however, my mother was pinned inside her new vehicle (Lexus) she had just purchased. My youngest brother jumped out of the car, running on his adrenaline because he anticipated on the car exploding.

He asked Josiah if he was ok and he responded yes, then he told him to jump out of the car. My brother, Mark, tried to assist my mother to the best of his ability. Mark had seen smoke coming from the car, so he thought for sure it was ready to BLOW! He finally realized that her door was totally smashed and there was no way to help her. Then, he got back into the vehicle and told her to lean towards him; he promised to get her out to safety. In the meantime, my mother saw a bright light. This light was a representation of the presence of the Lord and his protecting angels. Although, she could not see Mark she felt him pulling her out of the vehicle.

Mind you, Mark is about 6 feet 5 inches tall and he kept his promise. Mom leaned over to him and he pulled her out; however, he noticed her right wrist was broken and she suffered many cuts and bruises. He called out to mom to see if she was conscious and still with us. She responded and later said, "I saw a real bright light and then it vanished." She realized immediately it was purpose waiting! Always know that "PROBLEMS PRODUCE PAIN, PAIN PRODUCE PROMOTION, PROMOTION PRODUCE PURPOSE AND PURPOSE will lead you into your PROMISE."

Later, after being examined by the doctor, she was diagnosed with a fractured foot. Finally, after hospital appointments, examinations and numerous therapy visits; my mother, brother, and son were attending therapy sessions that lasted throughout the entire summer of 2014. This set us at the close of the 2013-2014 school year and in time for the 2014-2015 school year to begin.

I had to renew my contract! Therefore, I kept my pre-scheduled appointment and prepared for the new school year. To my surprise, I had received a PROMOTION! Somebody say, with PURPOSE comes PROMOTION!

I received a new opportunity to work as a Second Grade Teacher with more financial security. I have come to realize that whatever an earthly father will not do, our HEAVENLY FATHER will see to it getting done!

Besides, my father was a prime example of a provider for his family; however, my children are not able to attest the same about their earthly father, due to his lack of ability to provide. Yet, each one of them have decided to engage into an sincere and committed relationship with their Heavenly Father, God, through his son, Jesus, who gives them <u>all</u> Love, Joy, Peace, Longsuffering, Gentleness, Forgiveness, Goodness, Meekness, Temperance, and Faith.

I tell you the truth, knowing Jesus as not only a friend, but also Lord and Savior has given them hope for their present and future expectations, as well as mine. Purpose is provoking each of us to hold on, keep moving and never give up until we reach our higher ground!

Finally, I encourage you with this; do not allow the cares of this world to predict your outcome, but embrace the LIFE that will "provoke you to your purpose". **<u>PURPOSE IS WAITING ON YOU!</u>**

Journal 8
(The Open Door)

Name:_____ Date:_____

WORD SEARCH PUZZLE

LOST	UNEASY	FORSAKEN
STRONG	DISAPPOINTED	COURAGEOUS
ZEALOUS	TIRED	FRETFUL
AFRAID	REFRESH	WEARY
HAPPY	ANGRY	CONQUEROR
STUPID	WINNER	

CIRCLE ALL THE WORDS IN THIS PUZZLE THAT DEFINES WHO YOU ARE NOW!
**Focus on LETTING GO OF THE PAST, LIVE IN THE PRESENT AND MOVE FORWARD INTO YOUR FUTURE... THIS IS THE PROMISE AND PURPOSE FOR YOUR LIFE!!

WHO AM I?

M	H	K	M	M	Y	K	K	P	K	H	M	Y	T	I	P	F	M	H	R	R	Y	G	C
D	T	D	Y	Q	N	R	K	T	I	W	E	Q	H	Y	R	A	E	W	B	H	Y	S	U
E	T	E	I	Y	F	N	G	D	A	M	S	E	N	D	M	R	F	T	W	Q	J	K	G
T	M	C	A	U	W	C	Q	N	B	V	D	U	H	T	E	N	Y	U	S	J	M	N	D
N	A	S	Y	R	Y	H	D	N	A	T	O	Z	O	U	S	N	I	Y	M	O	V	G	V
I	A	Z	U	N	E	A	S	Y	O	H	F	S	M	E	G	P	O	L	A	P	L	E	J
O	P	R	B	I	C	H	D	V	Z	E	L	E	A	A	G	E	X	D	W	T	L	I	D
P	A	E	U	Q	W	H	W	X	Z	X	N	E	Y	X	L	A	N	P	N	I	E	G	X
P	L	F	S	H	H	J	O	J	P	I	S	I	I	C	J	Z	R	E	J	A	L	O	V
A	V	R	Y	T	A	I	E	U	T	S	R	T	O	F	W	U	O	U	D	F	B	Y	Q
S	D	E	L	E	N	F	Y	I	V	W	E	N	R	B	W	O	N	C	O	A	E	A	M
I	V	S	K	D	A	K	R	V	I	Z	Q	N	B	O	Y	B	V	I	Y	C	M	H	L
D	G	H	T	B	G	E	T	N	Y	U	J	Y	K	V	N	V	T	Q	T	O	K	J	E
Q	W	M	L	T	D	F	N	H	E	Q	Q	S	S	X	B	G	V	W	G	J	D	O	H
J	I	W	O	K	G	E	F	R	N	X	E	Z	E	Q	P	I	A	H	H	L	D	M	R
L	F	N	I	W	R	D	O	O	S	C	A	R	E	D	X	C	W	S	F	T	E	A	M
N	U	U	N	G	P	R	E	E	R	Y	I	D	P	E	Z	I	D	J	P	Q	U	S	R
O	X	F	R	V	E	Q	S	G	V	S	K	Y	B	M	A	S	B	I	X	I	U	E	Y
D	Y	S	T	V	L	X	D	W	T	J	A	N	D	H	U	N	N	O	A	O	Y	R	P
Z	Q	V	K	E	U	O	D	B	X	I	J	K	S	D	R	L	T	P	L	R	W	M	I
Q	Q	Q	O	V	R	K	H	S	R	W	G	T	E	H	N	R	E	A	L	I	F	D	C
H	C	U	Q	T	A	F	A	B	E	T	R	C	P	N	D	V	E	F	Z	S	Q	A	Z
X	F	S	T	U	P	I	D	Z	O	L	Y	P	P	A	H	Z	E	R	W	Q	Q	A	H
U	C	Z	L	W	P	O	N	V	W	A	U	R	M	G	I	T	M	D	E	U	M	F	U

Taken December 2014
Tulsa, OK

Taken June 5, 2016
Memphis, TN

Author's Update–

My children and I are currently residing with my mother and she is honored to have us as her company. My youngest brother, Mark, has decided to rearrange his living arrangements to be of support for our mother, my family, at my request and myself. He too, recognizes the need to be there for our mother, as well as, a mentor and man of integrity that my children so desperately desire to have around. My father was my children's mentor and after his passing, they felt a void deep within. No one can replace my father, because he had a close bond with my children that will always remain. However, having someone in their lives, as a mentor, helped them subside the pain and agony they often felt from the passing of their grandfather. All eight of us are doing well as we push the life and legacy of my late father's ministry. He was a very powerful man that touched many lives across the world. He had a vision and with God's help, it lives on. We miss him dearly; however, we know that if we walk upright before the Lord, we will meet again, according to Matthew 22:30.

My children are making me quite PROUD! They are all very gifted, intelligent and talented

God saw fit to elevate my oldest son, Princeton. He was en-rolled in the 8th grade for two weeks and started his third week as a 9ᵗʰ grader. He is 18 years of age now, and he graduated a year early, with many Honors, CLASS OF 2016. He is and always has been a very studios, and motivated young man. Moreover, he won 1ˢᵗ place in the Ebony Bowl (Black History) competition, while at-tending the 6ᵗʰ grade. Furthermore, he won 2ⁿᵈ place in a Talent Show, during his Junior High School years, where he performed an original piece on the piano. Both winnings were a monetary gift and/or gift card. He is an AWESOME SON! He holds many goals and aspirations that I pray will come into fruition. He is currently enrolled, as a student, at Oral Roberts University (ORU).

However, I would like to mention that he is a preacher, head musician/organist at our church, and future author. The release of his first CD was June 1, 2016. He is most definitely mature beyond his years. His spectacular and incredible art of music is coming soon to iTunes. For further information, you can contact him at pcdald1@hotmail.com

My son, Josiah, is very caring, loving and an athletic young man. He is now 16 years of age. He assists as the audio technician at our local church. His goal is to become a professional athlete and pursue the position of a Doctor or CPA. He is a very loving son with innovative ideas! He always tries to protect me and show some type of concern about my well-being, as well as, his family. He has promised to reach certain goals that will not leave his family, or I, in a state of lack ever again. I call him MILLIONAIRE MAN, because he is always trying to find a way to make progress and be successful.

My son, Jeremiah, is a precious young man. He often thinks outside the box. Through the years, I have noticed new talents. He is 14 years of age and he currently serves as our percussionist at our local church. He is a very talented drummer. In fact, neither he nor his brother, Princeton, has had music lessons. It is a pure gift from God. Of course, my extended family members are a very musically talented family. Jeremiah desires to be a very successful and professional athlete. In addition, he enjoys designing, architect, and computer literacy. Furthermore, he is very gifted with his hands. I have been trying to persuade him that becoming a physical therapist may be his area of interest, because he works miracles, in relieving unwanted pain, through his hands.

My son, Benjamin, is extremely talented. I refer to him as an All American Model. He and his twin sister are now 11 years old. He is an artist, singer, musician, and athlete. Benjamin's interest has always been in drawing. The gift was imparted from my father to me, to him. His level of artwork is simply amazing! He creates an authentic picture that tells a story. He is currently working on some opportunities to pursue his God-given talent, an artist. Some day he will be very famous for his creative ability to see what the normal eye does not envision. He is undeniably an innovator as well. He serves as a help to our ministry, Fellowship Church. He and his twin sister work faithfully as Praise and Worship singers.

My princess, Breanna, is a very beautiful encouraging young lady. She is also 11 years old and very intelligent. She really enjoys expressive dancing. She appears to hold the place of a songwriter, as well. Her wealth of knowledge and wisdom tends to amaze me. She is definitely, BORN TO WIN! Breanna enjoys writing books and songs in her spare time. Maybe one day she will publish some of her work. She is a natural beauty when it comes to modeling and I expect to see her move forward in whatever she puts her hands to do.

Mother

Leader

A Woman

Singer

Author

Made in the USA
Monee, IL
31 July 2020

37257281R00050